WORLD BANK WORKING PAPER NO. 18

Measuring Social Capital

An Integrated Questionnaire

Christiaan Grootaert
Deepa Narayan
Veronica Nyhan Jones
Michael Woolcock

THE WORLD BANK
Washington, D.C.

ISBN: 0-8213-5661-5
eISBN: 0-8213-5662-3
ISSN: 1726-5878

Christiaan Grootaert is Lead Economist in the Social Development Department at the World Bank. Deepa Narayan is Senior Advisor in the Poverty Reduction and Economic Management Network at the World Bank. Veronica Nyhan Jones is Research Analyst at the World Bank Institute. Michael Woolcock is Senior Social Scientist in the Development Research Group at the World Bank.

Library of Congress Cataloging-in-Publication Data
Measuring social capital: an integrated questionnaire/Christiaan Grootaert ... [et al.].
    p. cm. -- (World Bank working paper; no. 18)
  Includes bibliographical references.
  ISBN 0-8213-5661-5
    1. Social capital (Sociology)--Research--Methodology. 2. Questionnaires. I Grootaert, Christiaan, 1950- II. Series.

HM708 .M432003
302--dc22

                                                                        2003062509

TABLE OF CONTENTS

FOREWORD

To enhance its development effectiveness, the World Bank has, in recent years, taken an increasingly multidimensional approach to understanding the causes, manifestations, and consequences of poverty. In so doing, it has engaged in extensive conceptual, empirical, and policy-related work on social capital. This work has sought to provide more detailed insights regarding the various survival and mobility strategies of the poor, while also exploring the nature and extent of social relations between the households, associations and communities of poor people, on the one hand, and markets, states, and non-governmental organizations, on the other. It has subsequently informed major documents such as the *World Development Report 2000/01*, economic and sector work (e.g., country poverty assessments and strategy papers), new operational activities (e.g., empowerment and community-driven development), and individual household poverty surveys.

There have been many attempts to measure social capital at the project level as well as at the national level. The earliest stages of this work was of necessity carried out by teams of committed researchers and practitioners eager to rethink the role of social relations in development. As interest in and demand for tools to measure social capital has risen, however, so too has the rigor, coherence, and comparability of the various studies on which this interest draws. The survey tool presented in this publication—intended primarily for incorporation into household surveys of poverty—draws on the practical lessons from these earlier measurement initiatives. It has also benefited from detailed input from a team of external experts and has been piloted in two very different country settings (Albania and Nigeria), so in this sense represents the latest thinking of researchers both inside and outside the Bank. As such, however, it is the next rather than final step in attempts to refine and improve our understanding of local social contexts, and thus our collective capacity to respond more effectively to the interests and aspirations of the poor.

John Page
Director
Poverty Group
Poverty Reduction
 and Economic Management

Steen Jorgenson
Director
Social Development
Environmentally and Sustainability
 Sustainable Development

ABSTRACT

The idea of social capital has enjoyed a remarkable rise to prominence in both the theoretical and applied social science literature over the last decade. While lively debate has accompanied that journey, thereby helping to advance our thinking and to clarify areas of agreement and disagreement, much still remains to be done. One approach that we hope can help bring further advances for both scholars and practitioners is the provision of a set of empirical tools for measuring social capital.

The purpose of this paper is to introduce such a tool—the Integrated Questionnaire for the Measurement of Social Capital (SC-IQ)—with a focus on applications in developing countries. The tool aims to generate quantitative data on various dimensions of social capital as part of a larger household survey (such as the Living Standards Measurement Survey or a household income/expenditure survey). Specifically, six dimensions are considered: groups and networks; trust and solidarity; collective action and cooperation; information and communication; social cohesion and inclusion; empowerment and political action. The paper addresses sampling and data collection issues for implementing the SC-IQ and provides guidance for the use and analysis of data. The tool has been pilot-tested in Albania and Nigeria and a review of lessons learned is presented.

We hope that better empirical information on social capital will lead to greater dialogue between researchers, policymakers, task managers, and poor people themselves, thus ultimately leading to the design and implementation of more effective poverty reduction strategies.

PART I

INTRODUCTION

Purpose

The idea of social capital has enjoyed a remarkable rise to prominence in both the theoretical and applied social science literature over the last decade.[1] While lively debate has accompanied that journey, thereby helping to advance our thinking while clarifying areas of agreement and disagreement, much still remains to be done. One approach that we hope can help bring further advances for both scholars and practitioners is providing a set of empirical tools for measuring social capital. The purpose of this paper is to introduce such a tool with a focus on applications in developing countries. Some debates, of course, cannot be resolved empirically, and what one chooses to measure (or not) is itself necessarily a product of a particular set of guiding assumptions (see below). Nevertheless, conceptual debates cannot be resolved in an empirical vacuum. We hope our attempts to provide a basis for measuring different dimensions of social capital will encourage greater dialogue between researchers, policymakers, task managers, and poor people themselves. Through this dialogue, hopefully, knowledge of the social dimensions of economic development will improve, and with it our joint capacity to design and implement more effective poverty reduction strategies.

The purpose of the Integrated Questionnaire for the Measurement of Social Capital (SC-IQ) is to provide a core set of survey questions for those interested in generating quantitative data on various dimensions of social capital as part of a larger household survey (such as the Living Standards Measurement Survey). Each question included in this document is drawn from prior survey work on social capital (where it has demonstrated its reliability, validity, and usefulness). The document as a whole has been subject to extensive input and critique from an external panel of expert advisors,[2]

---

1. See Figure 1.1 in Isham, Kelly, and Ramaswamy (2002), which documents the exponentially rising number of citations to social capital in EconLit from 1993-2000.

2. We are grateful to Beatriz Ascarrunz, Michael Cassidy, Amrita Daniere, David Halpern, Roslyn Harper, John Helliwell, Kevin Karty, Lant Pritchett, Robert Putnam, Thierry van Bastelaer, and Ashutosh Varshney for serving as external advisors to this project. Our World Bank colleagues Nora Dudwick, Kathy Lindert, Steve Knack, and Diane Steele also provided very valuable input.

and has been pre-tested in the field (in Nigeria and Albania). We stress from the outset, however, that (a) not all listed questions are likely to be useful in all places; (b) not every phrasing of a particular question is likely to be appropriate in every context, and/or to translate easily into other languages; and (c) several locally-important issues may need to be added.

The majority of Living Standards Measurement Surveys are conducted at the national level, with a nationally representative sample, often in the context of a national-level poverty assessment. Adding a social capital module to such a survey opens up the possibility of studying the links between different dimensions of social capital and poverty. A few examples of such analysis are discussed in a section below. However, the application of the SC-IQ is not limited to national-level inquiries. There is much interest in social capital information in the context of the design and implementation of development projects, and the SC-IQ is useful for this purpose as well. If there is a desire to obtain baseline data on social capital prior to launching a project, the SC-IQ could be used in combination with other data collection at the project level aimed at providing a baseline of socio-economic information. Often such data is collected in anticipation of a future evaluation of the project's impact. Successful project evaluation requires multiple rounds of data collection. Adding the SC-IQ to each round of data collection would make it possible to assess the impact of the project on social capital, or conversely, to assess whether areas with high levels of social capital have more successful project implementation.

Audience and Background

The SC-IQ is designed for use by researchers, evaluators, and managers of projects and programs, those conducting poverty assessments or national social capital surveys, and those developing national poverty reduction strategies. It is especially designed for incorporation into other large household surveys, such as the Living Standards Measurement Survey (LSMS). Importantly, however, this tool is *not* for first-time researchers; it presumes a solid grasp of social research methods in general and survey research tools in particular, as well as familiarity with the core themes and debates in the social capital literature. This methodological and conceptual knowledge is needed to make the necessary in-context adjustments and modifications to the survey instrument suggested in the preceding section.

Though a survey tool is obviously designed to generate quantitative data, we are conscious that a rich tradition of social capital research has drawn on qualitative methods (for example, Narayan 2000, Grootaert and van Bastelaer 2002b). Indeed, a complementary qualitative tool is currently being developed, and in due course we hope to include both tools as part of a single package so that teams of researchers can combine their particular methodological skills[3] to construct a more comprehensive picture of the structures and perceptions of different dimensions of social capital (see below). For now, however, we present this quantitative tool on its own, given that, when used carefully, the form of data it can provide is often the most immediately useful (and persuasive) to policymakers, task managers, and researchers.

The primary material on which this survey is based brings together the lessons learned from the following studies (listed chronologically):

   ■ *The Tanzania Social Capital Survey* collected data on associational memberships and trust, and related this to access to services and agricultural technology (see Narayan and Pritchett 1999).
   ■ *The Local Level Institutions Study* collected comparable data on structural social capital in Bolivia, Burkina Faso and Indonesia. The analysis focused on the role of social capital in shaping household welfare and poverty, access to credit, and collective action (see Grootaert 2001).

---

3. On strategies for mixing qualitative and quantitative approaches in policy research and program evaluation, see Rao and Woolcock (2003).

▓ *The Social Capital Initiative* sponsored 12 studies on the role of social capital in sectoral projects and on the process of creation and destruction of social capital. The empirical lessons were brought together in two volumes (Grootaert and van Bastalaer 2002a, 2002b).

▓ *The Social Capital Survey* in Ghana and Uganda collected data on groups and networks, subjective well-being, political engagement, sociability, community activities, violence and crime, and communications (see Narayan and Cassidy 2001).

▓ *The Guatemala Poverty Assessment* combined an LSMS with a social capital module (World Bank 2003; see also Ibáñez, Lindert, and Woolcock 2002).[4]

Social Capital: A Conceptual Overview

In the contemporary academic literature, social capital is discussed in two related (but clearly different) ways.[5] The first, primarily associated with sociologists Ronald Burt, Nan Lin, and Alejandro Portes, refers to the resources (such as information, ideas, support) that individuals are able to procure by virtue of their relationships with other people. These resources ("capital") are "social" in that they are only accessible in and through these relationships, unlike physical (tools, technology) or human (education, skills) capital, for example, which are essentially the property of individuals. The structure of a given network—who interacts with whom, how frequently, and on what terms—thus has a major bearing on the flow of resources through that network. Those who occupy key strategic positions in the network, especially those whose ties span important groups, can be said to have more social capital than their peers, precisely because their network position gives them heightened access to more and better resources (Burt 2000).

The second (and more common) approach to social capital, one most closely associated with political scientist Robert Putnam, refers to the nature and extent of one's involvement in various informal networks and formal civic organizations. From chatting with neighbors or engaging in recreational activities to joining environmental organizations and political parties, social capital in this sense is used as a conceptual term to characterize the many and varied ways in which a given community's members interact. So understood, it is possible to conduct a map of a community's associational life, and thus with it a sense of the state of its civic health. A range of social problems—crime, health, poverty, unemployment—have been linked empirically to a community's endowment of social capital (or lack thereof), and with them a sense of concern among citizens and policymakers alike that new forms of social capital must be imagined and constructed as other or older forms decline (for example, as a result of technological or demographic change). These issues are relevant to both high and low income countries.

Scholars working in both conceptual traditions agree that it is important to recognize that social capital is not a single entity, but is rather multi-dimensional in nature. Given that social capital is most frequently defined in terms of the groups, networks, norms, and trust that people have available to them for productive purposes, the survey tool in this paper has been designed to capture this multi-dimensionality, exploring (a) the *types* of groups and networks that poor people can call upon, and the nature and extent of their contributions to other members of those groups and networks. The survey also explores (b) respondents' subjective *perceptions* of the trustworthiness of other people and key institutions that shape their lives, as well as the norms of cooperation and reciprocity that surround attempts to work together to solve problems.[6]

---

4. This work also drew upon research on survival and mobility strategies in Delhi slums (Jha, Rao, and Woolcock 2002).

5. Woolcock and Narayan (2000) discuss four broad perspectives connecting social capital to development outcomes; the dual distinction posed here refers to the core definitions as applied across a range of substantive fields.

6. The distinction between (a) and (b) is sometimes referred to as, respectively, 'structural' and 'cognitive' social capital (e.g., Krishna and Uphoff, 2002).

In its attempt to measure network access and forms of participation, the survey also adopts the common distinction between "bonding" social capital—ties to people who are similar in terms of their demographic characteristics, such as family members, neighbors, close friends and work colleagues—and "bridging" social capital—ties to people who do not share many of these characteristics (Gittell and Vidal 1998, Narayan 2002, Putnam 2000). What defines the boundaries between different bonding and bridging groups will clearly vary across contexts (and is thus endogenous), but these boundaries are salient nonetheless—usually politically—and it is important to identify where they lie, and how they are constructed and maintained.

In recent years, some scholars have suggested a third conceptual classification. Called "linking" social capital (Woolcock 1999, World Bank 2000), this dimension refers to one's ties to people in positions of authority, such as representatives of public (police, political parties) and private (banks) institutions. This conceptual development stemmed from a long-standing concern that there can be (and usually is) enormous heterogeneity—both demographically and in terms of their importance to one's immediate or future well-being—among the people that could plausibly be identified as part of one's bridging social capital portfolio. Where bridging social capital, as the metaphor suggests, is essentially horizontal (that is, connecting people with more or less equal social standing), linking social capital is more vertical, connecting people to key political (and other) resources and economic institutions—that is, across power differentials. Importantly, it is not the mere presence of these institutions (schools, banks, insurance agencies) that constitutes linking social capital, but rather the nature and extent of *social* ties between clients and providers, many of which are an inherent medium for delivering those services (such as teaching, agricultural extension, general practice medicine, etc.).[7] So defined, access to linking social capital is demonstrably central to well-being, especially in poor countries and communities, where too often bankers charge usurious interest rates, the police are corrupt, and teachers fail to show up for work (Narayan 2000). Local leaders and intermediaries able to facilitate connections between poor communities and external development assistance (including government programs—Krishna 2002) constitute an important source of linking social capital.

It is also important to recognize, however, that these different forms of social capital, like human capital, can be used for purposes that hinder rather than help an individual's welfare (Portes 1998, Woolcock 1998)—for example, when group membership norms confer obligations to share rather than accumulate wealth, or deny members access to services (such as preventing girls from going to school). Absent other forms of control and accountability, linking social capital can also quickly become nepotistic or a mechanism for insider-trading and political favoritism. As such, a key empirical and policy question is therefore what institutional conditions and/or combinations of different dimensions of social capital generate outcomes that serve the public good.

While acknowledging the strengths of different views on social capital in the literature, it is not the purpose of the survey instrument in this paper to resolve these debates per se, but rather to provide a range of pre-tested survey questions that can help researchers and practitioners alike move towards greater clarity on the basis of the evidence. As such, it emphasizes the different types of networks and organizations to which household members have access, and gives particular attention to understanding the processes by which inclusion in (or exclusion from) them is sustained. It also includes more subjective questions such as those pertaining to perceptions of trust (in neighbors, service providers, etc.), normative reciprocity, and collective action.[8]

---

7. On this point see Pritchett and Woolcock (forthcoming).

8. We also recognize that social capital has been conceived and measured at different units of analysis, from individuals (Glaeser, Laibson and Sacerdote, 2002, Collier 2002) and households through to regions and entire societies (Fukuyama 1995). As this survey tool demonstrates, we believe social capital is most accurately captured at the household level, asking questions of individuals as *members of various social groups*. Broader measures of social capital are valid only to the extent they are drawn from appropriate representative samples of households.

The SC-IQ's Six Dimensions

Within a conceptual framework of social capital based at the household level, it is still important to recognize that there are a host of substantive issues on which relevant information can be obtained. On the basis of previous survey work on social capital, our reading of the literature, and the input from our advisory group, we have elected to arrange this material into six broad sections:

Groups and Networks. This is the category most commonly associated with social capital. The questions here consider the nature and extent of a household member's participation in various types of social organizations and informal networks, and the range of contributions that one gives and receives from them. It also considers the diversity of a given group's membership, how its leadership is selected, and how one's involvement has changed over time.

Trust and Solidarity. In addition to the canonical trust question asked in a remarkable number of cross-national surveys, this category seeks to procure data on trust towards neighbors, key service providers, and strangers, and how these perceptions have changed over time.

Collective Action and Cooperation. This category explores whether and how household members have worked with others in their community on joint projects and/or in response to a crisis. It also considers the consequences of violating community expectations regarding participation.

Information and Communication. Access to information is being increasingly recognized as central to helping poor communities have a stronger voice in matters affecting their well-being (World Bank 2002). This category of questions explores the ways and means by which poor households receive information regarding market conditions and public services, and the extent of their access to communications infrastructure.

Social Cohesion and Inclusion. "Communities" are not single entities, but rather are characterized by various forms of division and difference that can lead to conflict. Questions in this category seek to identify the nature and extent of these differences, the mechanisms by which they are managed, and which groups are excluded from key public services. Questions pertaining to everyday forms of social interaction are also considered.

Empowerment and Political Action. Individuals are "empowered" to the extent they have a measure of control over institutions and processes directly affecting their well-being (World Bank 2002). The questions in this section explore household members' sense of happiness, personal efficacy, and capacity to influence both local events and broader political outcomes.

The survey instrument thus reflects the group membership ("structural") and subjective perceptions of trust and norms ("cognitive") dimensions of social capital (sections 1 and 2), the main ways in which social capital operates (sections 3 and 4), and major areas of application or outcomes (sections 5 and 6). Specific suggestions regarding procedures for analyzing the data from each of the six sections is provided in the "Suggestions for Data Analysis" section below.

Sampling and Data Collection Issues

Although social capital has been conceptualized at the micro, meso and macro levels, the tools needed to measure social capital at the level of households or individuals are very different from those needed to measure social capital at the country level. The SC-IQ focuses on measurement at the micro level—that is, at the level of households and individuals. This corresponds to the focus of the Living Standards Measurement Surveys (LSMS), which aim to measure living standards of households and individuals. This correspondence in focus makes it possible to integrate the SC-IQ easily into the LSMS.

When the SC-IQ is used as a module for the LSMS, all sampling and data collection issues will be addressed in the context of the LSMS. For example, decisions about sample size and sample selection method will be made for the LSMS at large, and will apply to the SC-IQ in the same way as they do for all other survey modules. A living standards measurement survey is typically conducted over a sample of 1500 to 5000 households. This sample size is sufficient to allow various types of disaggregated data analysis (by region, socio-economic group, gender, etc.). The potential thus exists to undertake a similarly disaggregated analysis of the social capital information.

Because it was designed to be a module for the LSMS, the SC-IQ does not collect data on social capital at the level of the community. All questions are addressed to individuals, in the context of a household survey, and the objective is to obtain information about the participation of household members in groups and associations, perceptions of trust and empowerment, household participation in collective action, etc. Some of the questions do ask about the respondent's perception of certain community attributes, such as the community's ability to come together to cope with calamities or to address issues of common concern. This is different of course from obtaining community-level data on social capital, such as the density of associational life or the frequency of community collective action.

In some applications of the SC-IQ, it may be useful to supplement the household level information with community data on social capital. This will often be possible if the SC-IQ is conducted as part of an LSMS, because many living standards measurement surveys add a community module. In such cases, a number of questions on social capital issues could be added to this community module. Because the LSMS community module is typically fairly limited in size, it will be necessary to be very selective in choosing the social capital questions to be added.[9] A good source for selecting these questions is the community questionnaire that is part of the Social Capital Assessment Tool (SOCAT). The SOCAT is a broader instrument for collecting data on social capital at the level of households, communities and organizations[10] (Grootaert and van Bastelaer 2000b).

Adaptation and Pilot Testing of the SC-IQ

The SC-IQ presented in this paper is a prototype instrument. It tries to strike a balance between conceptual rigor and cross-cultural flexibility and adaptability. Although the design and content of the SC-IQ is based on a wide experience of collecting social capital data in different countries, any application will require adaptation to the local setting. Users should be guided in this process by giving serious consideration to the specific purposes for which the survey will be used, and the particular audience to whom one is seeking to communicate the eventual findings. These considerations will influence the type, complexity, and number of questions included in the final survey, the sophistication (and associated expense) of the data analysis, and the style of language employed to interpret and disseminate the findings. Though time and budgetary pressures may cause temptations to adopt the questions and format outlined here "as is," we strongly recommend that all users allow adequate time and resources for ensuring that the purpose of the research is clear, as are the procedures for designing, formatting, and pre-testing selected questions, and analyzing the data to which they will give rise. These points were underscored during field tests of this survey in Albania and Nigeria during summer 2002.

As a practical matter, adaptation is a three-step process. First, a general review is necessary of the six different modules in the SC-IQ and an assessment needs to be made whether the balance between the different topics is appropriate for the proposed application. For example, it is quite possible that for a given application, issues of trust and solidarity are more important than those

---

9. The design and typical content of the LSMS community module is discussed in Grosh and Glewwe (2000).

10. In the SOCAT, community data on social capital are collected by means of community focus groups as well as a structured community questionnaire. The collected information pertains to community assets, community governance, collective action, the density of local organizations, and the relationships among organizations and between organizations and the community.

relating to the density of organizations and networks. In such a case, it would be legitimate for the survey designers to expand the module on Trust and Solidarity and, in order not to extend the overall length of the survey, to reduce the scope of the module on Groups and Networks accordingly. It would not be legitimate, however, to completely eliminate the Groups and Network module, because this would undercut the conceptual framework that underlies the SC-IQ and thus reduce the analytic potential of the collected data. The pilot survey of the SC-IQ in Nigeria brought to light, for example, that households in that country belong to many more groups (as much as 50) than is the case in most other countries. Therefore, it was suggested that the list of possible organizations and the follow-up questions be reduced and more targeted to the prime organizations of interest, so as to not unduly lengthen the interview time. In contrast, the pilot survey in Albania indicated the need to add to the prototype list country-specific organizations such as the "fis," a particular form of family network which is very important in Albanian society.

The second step of the adaptation process consists of a detailed review of the questions and the answer codes to see if they are relevant in the local context. Because a survey uses closed-ended questions, it can be difficult to anticipate and account for the range of responses and interpretations across local contexts. For example, several questions in modules 1 and 3 ask how the respondent would react in hypothetical situations which would typically require trust in or collaboration with other community members. The chosen situations need to have a realistic chance of occurring in the daily environment of the respondent. Where crop failures are a common occurrence, it makes sense to ask respondents whether community members would get together to deal with this calamity or would act individually. If crop failures are rare, another hypothetical calamity should be selected to assess the community's willingness to work together. Likewise, in module 5 dealing with social cohesion, a list of characteristics is suggested that may be the cause for exclusion. This should contain only characteristics for which there is local variation. In situations where there is no ethnic diversity, there is no point in asking whether differences in ethnic backgrounds can be the cause for exclusion

It is equally important that the questions and response options be culturally sensitive. For example, a question in the sociability section asks with what frequency people meet outside the home for food and/or drinks. The pilot survey revealed that in some parts of Nigeria, where people are not supposed to take alcohol for religious reasons, the term "drink" was interpreted to mean alcohol and caused unnecessary embarrassment among respondents. This situation needs to be distinguished though from questions which cause discomfort but are necessary, such as political action questions.

The third step concerns language. The prototype SC-IQ was drafted in English, and thus application in most countries will require translation into local languages. Specific attention needs to be paid to the translation of frequently used terms in the questionnaire, e.g., organization, network, trust, exclusion, collective action, etc. Past experience has shown that translation of such terms is not always easy, and, if necessary, local sociologists and language experts may need to be consulted. Once agreement is reached on a dictionary of the main terms, the actual questionnaire can be translated into the local languages. For example, in the Nigerian pilot exercise, the researchers struggled to translate the terms "get along" and "togetherness" into Hausa, Ibo and Yoruba languages. Also, one of the questions on trust which offers the responses "most people can be trusted" versus "you can't be too careful" proved difficult to translate accurately.

Although the SC-IQ is not a very long questionnaire, translation can still be an expensive exercise, especially when there are multiple local languages, and there may be a temptation to skip this step. However, we advise strongly against not translating the questionnaires. Experience indicates that when enumerators are forced to translate on the fly (during the interviews), many inconsistencies arise in the translation and the flow of the interview is slowed down. The end result can be a significant reduction in the quality and comparability of the collected information. The only obvious exception to this situation is when the local language is non-written, as is the case for example with some Caribbean *patois*. In that case, the training will need to allocate additional time to train enumerators in the translation and to allow them time to practice.

To ensure accuracy of the translated instruments, it is recommended that all instruments be back-translated into English. The comparison of this translation with the original instruments is the most effective way to detect errors in translation.

After adapted and translated questionnaires are available, the survey teams need to be trained. The training needs to ensure that all enumerators adopt a similar protocol for (a) selecting households (and household respondents), (b) taking respondents through the inventory of questions, (c) filling out the survey, (d) responding to any substantive or procedural questions, and (e) clarifying (known) ambiguities. The more rigorous and comprehensive the up-front training, the higher is the likelihood of generating useable and useful data.

The final phase of preparation for the field work consists of a pilot test to assess all aspects of data collection. The sites for the pilot test should not include communities that would be part of the sample for the administration of the actual survey. The purpose of the pilot test is to administer the questionnaire in as many different geographic and socio-economic environments as possible, covering the range of situations one is likely to encounter during the actual application of the SC-IQ. Thus the selection of sites should not be random, but purposive and aim to ensure a balance between urban and rural communities, mountains and coastal communities, poor and rich areas, and areas of different ethnicity and language. Likewise, at the household level, a balance will be sought between male and female respondents, poor and rich households, and households from different occupational and ethnic backgrounds. The actual relevant criteria are of course location-specific. There are no hard rules about the optimal sample size for the pilot test, but past experience suggests that a sample of 200 to 300 households, spread over 10 to 20 communities, is adequate. More important than the precise sample size is the inclusion of different types of communities and respondents. For the pilot test in Albania, 257 surveys were completed across 16 villages, representing three diverse regions of the country. In Nigeria, a total of 300 households were interviewed in the country; in each of the three selected states (Adamawa, Enugu, and Osun), five towns were visited with 20 people surveyed in each town.[11]

The objective of the pilot exercise is to test the applicability of the questionnaire, to learn the time it takes to complete it in the local setting, and to fine-tune the logistics of the survey. The results from the pilot test may lead to modifications in the wording of questions, adjustments to the workload of the field teams, and other improvements in the implementation and management of the field work. As it is based on a non-representative sample, the data collected by the pilot test are not really suitable for analysis (except perhaps to test the data entry and tabulation program) and should never be merged with the data collected during the actual SC-IQ application.

The pilot applications of the SC-IQ helped to settle several issues which will facilitate the fieldwork. For example, questions seeking to uncover trends or changes over time proved difficult for many respondents and may become easier if reference is made to pivotal local events. Rather than asking generally about changes since five years ago, in Nigeria one might ask about pre- versus post-democracy. In Albania, one might frame the question in terms of pre- versus post-influx of refugees from Kosovo. These kinds of local adaptations will make it easier for the respondents to reply accurately and consistently. There were also mixed experiences with the questions involving scaled responses. Many respondents had difficulties distinguishing between, for example, "somewhat likely" and "somewhat unlikely." The use of a 1-to-5 scale helped in some cases but not all. This led to reformulation of the response options and the way the scales were formulated.

---

11. Annex A contains a detailed discussion of these pilot tests.

A final issue for which the pilot test may be helpful pertains to the way answers like "don't know/not sure" are coded and "not applicable" situations are dealt with (such as a question about who would take care of your children posed to a childless household). There are two ways to do this. Each question can have two additional explicit codes to cover the situations of no response and non-applicability. This makes, however, the questionnaire much longer. The alternative is to instruct the enumerators to use standardized codes for these two situations, applicable to all questions. These should be codes that are never used otherwise (for example, "88" for no answer and "99" for non-applicable). As this affects both the field work and the data entry, the pilot experiences from both activities should be considered in making a final choice.

Suggestions for Data Analysis[12]

As explained above, the SC-IQ was designed in part to be integrated into a broader survey such as the LSMS, but for certain applications it can be used as a standalone survey. In either case, it makes sense to start the analysis by looking at the social capital data on their own. The objective of this is to inventory existing social capital, to map the distribution of social capital across areas or socio-economic groups, and to gain a better insight into the different dimensions of social capital. However, more often than not, the analytic objective will also be to relate social capital to outcome variables such as household welfare and poverty, access to services, or general development indicators. This type of analysis is only possible of course when the SC-IQ is included in an LSMS or similar survey.

The first type of analysis will be primarily tabular in nature, and, given the content of the SC-IQ, be centered on three basic sets of indicators of social capital: membership in associations and networks (structural social capital), trust and adherence to norms (cognitive social capital), and collective action (an output measure). Tabular analysis is a simple and convenient way to organize data and to extract the basic messages that the data contain. In the case of the SC-IQ, these basic messages pertain to the extent social capital is observed across different types of households and the main characteristics or dimensions of this social capital. As the earlier conceptual discussion has made clear, the analysis of the dimensions of social capital should be anchored in the distinctions between structural and cognitive social capital and between bonding, bridging, and linking social capital. Some parts of the household information can also be aggregated at the level of the community and cross-tabulated by different characteristics of the community.

The main limitation of tabular analysis is that only a few variables can be tabulated at once, making it difficult to discern social capital's contribution to the welfare of the household or to other development outcome variables. The second part of the analysis will therefore need to include econometric analysis, in particular the estimation of multivariate models of household welfare. Such models aim to identify the contribution of social capital to monetary and non-monetary aspects of household welfare (consumption of goods, health, and education) in relation to other household assets such as land, human and physical capital. A key concern in this type of analysis is the direction of causality: does social capital make higher household welfare possible, or does higher household welfare allow the acquisition of more social capital?

Extensive empirical work has revealed three useful proxies for measuring social capital in a policy-relevant manner. The first of these is memberships in local associations and networks, and can be derived from module 1 of the SC-IQ. This indicator of structural social capital is based on the density of associations and the incidence of household memberships. Various aspects of membership (such as internal diversity) and institutional functioning (such as the extent of democratic decision making) are also relevant indicators. In the case of networks, which are less formal, the key information is the scope of the network and the internal diversity of membership.

---

12. This section draws heavily from chapter 3 in Grootaert and van Bastelaer (2002b).

The second set of proxy variables consists of indicators of trust and solidarity, which capture cognitive social capital, and which can be derived from module 2 of the SC-IQ. These measures are based on respondents' expectations about and experiences with behavior requiring trust. An important aspect of this is the extent to which households received or would receive assistance from members of their community or network in case of need.

Indicators of collective action constitute the third set of variables to capture social capital, and can be extracted from module 3 of the SC-IQ. The provision of many services requires collective action by a group of individuals. The extent to which this collective action occurs can be measured and is an indicator of underlying social capital (at least to the extent that the cooperation is not imposed by an external force, such as the government).

As proxies, these three types of indicators measure social capital from different vantage points. Membership in local associations and networks is clearly an input indicator, because the associations and networks are the vehicles through which social capital can be accumulated. This indicator resembles the use of years of schooling as a proxy for human capital. Trust can be seen as an input or output indicator, or even as a direct measure of social capital, depending upon one's conceptual approach. Collective action is an output indicator. Because of their different perspectives, it is recommended that these three types of indicators be tabulated and analyzed together, in order to provide a fuller picture of social capital and its impacts.

While modules 1 to 3 of the SC-IQ provide the information to calculate the three basic measures of social capital, modules 4 to 6 collect data that make it possible to examine in more depth certain aspects or manifestations of social capital. Module 4 gathers data on the sources of information and communication available to the members of the community. Modules 5 and 6 look at two important outcomes of social capital: social cohesion and inclusion, and empowerment and political action.

Maintaining and enhancing social capital depends critically on the ability of the members of a community to communicate among each other, with other communities and with members of their networks that live outside the community. Module 4 therefore inquires about the availability of a number of important means of communication and sources of information: post office, telephone, newspaper, radio and television. Because person-to-person contact is probably the most important form of direct communication, the module also inquires about the extent of travel and whether the respondent's house is accessible by road all year long.

The extent of social cohesion and inclusion is one of the most important positive outcomes of the presence of social capital in a community. Module 5 looks in detail at several aspects of this. Inclusion is assessed in the context of access to important services, such as education, health and justice. Where people are excluded from services, the reasons are probed and the severity of the exclusion is assessed, particularly whether the situation has ever led to violence. The overall level of conflict and violence in the community is also assessed in a subjective matter, i.e. by the perceptions of the respondents regarding safety and fear of becoming the victim of crime. On the positive side, a high level of sociability typically characterizes a socially cohesive community; as such, module 5 contains an extensive series of questions about every-day social interactions.

Lastly, module 6 examines the extent to which respondents feel empowered and participate in political action. While empowerment is a broad concept, the focus in the SC-IQ is on control over decisions that directly affect everyday life. The questionnaire asks about a number of concrete ways in which people may have attempted to improve this control, such as petitions to government officials, participation in public meetings, and participation in elections. As the willingness to undertake these types of actions is affected by perceptions of honesty of government officials and the extent of corruption, a few basic questions to assess this are included.

We will now provide a few suggestions for the tabular analysis of each of the six modules of the SC-IQ, followed by a brief discussion of multivariate analysis.

Groups and Networks

Social capital helps to disseminate information, reduces opportunistic behavior, and facilitates collective decision-making. The effectiveness with which structural social capital, in the form of the associations and networks, fulfills this role depends upon many aspects of these groups, reflecting their structure, their membership, and the way they function. The SC-IQ makes it possible to describe organizations along four key dimensions: the density of membership, the diversity of membership, the extent of democratic functioning, and the extent of connections to other groups.

At the level of households, the density of membership is measured by the average number of memberships of each household in existing organizations (this can be normalized by household size). This basic indicator can be cross-tabulated by location (region, province, urban/rural) or socio-economic characteristics of the household (income group, age and gender of the head of household, religion, ethnic group) to capture the distribution of memberships. The indicator can also be broken down by type of organization. A functional classification focuses on the prime objective of the association (education, health, credit, etc.). Another useful classification refers to the scope of the group: whether groups operate only in the community, are affiliated with other groups (inside or outside the community), or are part of a federated structure. Groups with linkages often have better access to resources, especially from outside the community, such as from government or NGOs. Using information on memberships, organizations can also be classified as to whether they represent primarily bonding, bridging, or linking social capital (World Bank 2000).

The SC-IQ data make it possible to assess the internal diversity of organizations according to nine criteria: kinship, religion, gender, age, ethnicity/linguistic group, occupation, education, political affiliation, and income level. Diversity information can be used separately or combined in an index. For example, a "diversity score" can be calculated for each organization, ranging from 0 to 9. These scores can be averaged over all or the most important organizations to which households belong. It is not immediately obvious whether a high degree of internal diversity is a positive or negative factor from the point of view of social capital. One could argue, on the one hand, that an internally homogeneous association would make it easier for members to trust each other, to share information, and to reach decisions. On the other hand, these members may also have similar information so that less would be gained from exchanging information. Furthermore, the coexistence of a series of associations that are each internally homogeneous but along different criteria could render the decision making process at the community level more difficult. Analysis in several countries has suggested that internally diverse associations yield higher levels of benefits than others, although homogeneous associations make it easier to bring about collective action (Grootaert 1999, 2001).

Organizations that follow a democratic pattern of decision-making are generally believed to be more effective than others. An indicator that measures participation in decision-making can therefore round out the set of indicators on structural social capital. This can be done on the basis of questions 1.15 to 1.17. Answers to these questions can be tabulated separately by type of organization (to assess whether certain categories of organizations are more democratic than others) or against spatial or socio-economic variables (to assess whether organizations in certain parts of the country tend to function more democratically, or whether organizations of the poor function differently from those of the rich). The questions can also be combined in a "democratic functioning score" in a similar way as the calculation of the diversity score.

Regarding networks, the SC-IQ provides three items of information: the size of the network, its internal diversity and the extent to which it would provide assistance in case of need. Because "network" is a difficult concept to define concretely in the context of a household survey, a pragmatic approach has been taken: a network is seen as a circle of "close friends"—that is, people one feels at ease with, can talk to about private matters, or call upon for help. The size of the network then is captured by the number of such close friends. The usefulness of the network is assessed by asking the respondents whether they could turn to the network in a series of hypothetical emergency situations. The answers to these questions can be aggregated to yield a "mutual support score" for the network. Diversity is assessed in a simpler way than was the case for associations, by focusing only on whether the network consists of people with different economic status. This is a key feature to determine the network's ability to provide resources to the respondent in case of need, and thus the network's usefulness in the management of risk.

Trust and Solidarity

Measurement of cognitive social capital in the SC-IQ is organized around the themes of trust and solidarity. Trust is an abstract concept that is difficult to measure in the context of a household questionnaire, in part because it may mean different things to different people. The SC-IQ approach therefore focuses both on generalized trust (the extent to which one trusts people overall) and on the extent of trust in specific types of people. Trust is also viewed in the context of specific transactions, such as lending and borrowing. Because of the difficulties in measuring trust, the questions in this section have a degree of redundancy to them. In part, this serves the purpose of cross-validating the responses to different questions. It is possible to tabulate the answers to each trust question against the usual spatial or socio-economic characteristics, but because of the complexity of the concept of trust, it is recommended to use factor analysis or principal component analysis to identify any underlying common factors across the different questions. This approach has been successfully used in empirical work. For example, a study on trust in Uganda found that from a series of questions on trust, three factors emerged which identified three different dimensions of trust: trust in agencies, trust in members of one's immediate environment and trust in the business community (Narayan and Cassidy 2001).

Collective Action and Cooperation

Collective action is the third basic type of proxy indicator for measuring social capital. The usefulness of this indicator stems from the fact that in the vast majority of settings, collective action is possible only if a significant amount of social capital is available in the community. The major exception occurs in totalitarian societies where the government can force people to work together on infrastructure projects or other types of common activities. Thus, the validity of the collective action indicator as a measure of social capital needs to be evaluated against the political context of a society. The indicators of structural and cognitive social capital discussed previously can be helpful here. Collective action is an important aspect of community life in many countries, although the purposes of the action may differ widely. In some countries, collective action consists primarily of community-organized activities for building and maintaining infrastructure and for providing related public services. In other countries, collective action is more politically oriented and used primarily to lobby elected officials to provide more services to the community.

The collective action section of the SC-IQ aims to collect three items of information: the extent of collective action, the type of the activities undertaken collectively, and an overall assessment of the extent of willingness to cooperate and participate in collective action. Each of these variables can be cross-tabulated against the usual set of spatial and socio-economic variables to obtain a pattern of the incidence of collective action. More interestingly perhaps is the cross-tabulation of collective action variables against the indicators of structural and cognitive social capital discussed previously. This would reveal whether communities with a high density of organizations and/or high levels of trust also display higher levels of collective action. Any correlations revealed by such tabulations could usefully be the subject of further multivariate analysis.

Information and Communication

Module 4 of the SC-IQ has a simple structure: it is a list of sources of information and means of communication. Analysis of this information is equally straightforward. Each item can be cross-tabulated separately against spatial and socio-economic variables to identify whether certain areas or groups have better or worse access to information and communication. The identified pattern can be compared against the pattern of structural and cognitive social capital established on the basis of the previous modules. If areas of low social capital are found to have poor access to information and communication, a further inquiry into possible causality might be warranted.

The information from module 4 can also be aggregated, either at the household level or at the community level, to obtain a single score for information and communication access. Factor analysis or principal component analysis are suitable techniques to that effect. Two questions, however, should be analyzed separately because they ask about sources of specific items of information: government activities (question 4.7) and market information (question 4.8). These questions serve two purposes. First, they make possible an assessment of the relative importance of groups and networks as sources for important information compared to "impersonal" sources such as newspapers or television. Second, because information on government activities and markets is directly relevant for the generation of income and/or for non-monetary aspects of well-being, it can be included as an explanatory variable in multivariate analysis of household well-being.

Social Cohesion and Inclusion

Module 5 of the SC-IQ brings together three related topics: inclusion, sociability, and conflict and violence. The section on inclusion ranges from general perceptions of social unity and togetherness of the community to specific experiences with exclusion. The respondent is first asked whether there are any divisions in the community and, if so, what characteristics cause it. Questions on exclusion from services at the level of the community are followed by more direct questions, such as whether the respondent has ever been the victim of exclusion. The most policy-relevant information will come from the detailed cross-tabulation of the presence of exclusion by type of service against the characteristics deemed to be the grounds for exclusion. This tabulation will reveal whether exclusion exists across the board, due to characteristics such as gender or ethnicity, or if the reasons for exclusion vary by type of service or activity. Such information has a high diagnostic value in identifying sources of social stress in the community. To compare the incidence of exclusion across communities, an "exclusion score" can be constructed by adding up the answers from several questions. For example, the five sub-answers from question 5.6 use a common scale and can easily be aggregated.

One of the positive manifestations of a high level of social capital in the community is the occurrence of frequent every-day social interactions. This "sociability" can take the form of meetings with people in public places, visits to other people's homes or visits from others into one's own home, and participation in community events such as sports or ceremonies. The section on sociability in module 5 covers each of these situations. In order to distinguish whether these daily social interactions are of the bonding or bridging variety, questions are asked whether the people with whom one meets are of the same or a different ethnic or linguistic group, economic status, social status, or religious group. The diversity of social interactions can usefully be compared to the diversity of the membership of associations (covered in module 1). Put together, these two items of information on diversity give a good picture of the internal divisiveness or cohesiveness of a community and whether bonding or bridging social capital predominates.

The presence of conflict in a community or in a larger area is often an indicator of the lack of trust or the lack of appropriate structural social capital to resolve conflicts, or both. The SC-IQ brings together three important items of information on conflict and violence: the extent and trend of violence, the contribution made by internal divisiveness in the community, and the feelings of insecurity stemming from fear of crime and violence. To match perceptions with fact, the four final questions in this module ask about the household's recent experience of crime. It is useful to tabulate this information both at the household level and the community level. It is quite likely that perceptions of violence as well as experience of it differ between rich and poor households, old and young people, etc. Likewise, different communities can have vastly different experiences with conflict and violence, even if they are geographically close. The comparison of communities will be made easier if the different questions on conflict and violence in module 5 are aggregated, either directly or by means of factor analysis.

Empowerment and Political Action

The final section of the SC-IQ takes a broad view that transcends social capital. Empowerment refers to the expansion of assets and capabilities of people to participate in, negotiate with, influence, control, and hold accountable institutions that affect their lives (World Bank 2002). Empowerment is brought about by a wide range of actions, such as making state institutions more responsive to poor people, removing social barriers, and building social opportunity (World Bank 2000). Empowerment is thus a broader concept than social capital, and political action is only one of many activities that can be undertaken to increase empowerment.

In the context of the SC-IQ, empowerment is defined more narrowly as the ability to make decisions that affect everyday activities and may change the course of one's life. Respondents are asked to assess this ability directly in question 6.2 to 6.4. As discussed above, political action is one venue to increase this ability. Module 6 considers a number of concrete political activities such as filing petitions, attending public meetings, meeting with politicians, participating in demonstrations and campaigns, and voting in elections. The analysis of this information can follow a pattern similar to that recommended for the previous module. The data can be aggregated both at the level of the household and the level of the community. Different households, depending upon their demographic, economic and social characteristics, will feel differently empowered and will participate in political action to differing degrees. It is useful to compare this pattern of empowerment with the patterns of access to information, fear of violence, sociability, and other dimensions of social capital derived from other modules. By the same token, earlier analysis will already have provided a community score of social cohesiveness and inclusion, and this information can usefully be complemented with a community score of empowerment and political action.

Multivariate Analysis: Social Capital and Household Welfare

The tabulations proposed so far had as their main purpose the mapping of the different dimensions of social capital across spatial and socio-economic characteristics. For the most part, these tabulations drew only or primarily on the data collected through the SC-IQ itself. A number of important policy questions can only be addressed by multivariate analysis and by combining data from the SC-IQ and the LSMS. These questions include:

- What is the contribution of social capital to household well-being, i.e. are households with higher level of social capital, as measured by the various indicators proposed so far, better off?
- What is the importance of social capital for poverty reduction?
- What are the determinants of social capital?

These questions address the role of social capital in the poverty reduction strategy set forth by the *World Development Report 2000/2001* (World Bank 2000). The first question focuses on the role of social capital in creating opportunities for enhancing income and improving other dimensions of well-being such as health and education. This includes the extent to which social capital improves access to credit and thus contributes to reducing vulnerability. The second question looks at the relative importance of social capital in the asset portfolio of poor households. The third question addresses the critical issue of building social capital, a core element of the empowerment pillar of the *World Development Report's* poverty reduction strategy.

Analyzing the contribution of social capital to household well-being can be done in the context of a simple conceptual framework which views social capital as one class of assets available to households for generating income and making consumption possible. The household has an asset endowment consisting of physical assets (land, equipment, cattle, etc.), human capital (years of schooling and work experience), and social capital. The household combines these assets to engage in productive activities, either in enterprises within the household or in the external labor market. This model can be formalized in a set of structural equations making up a conventional model of household economic behavior under constrained utility maximization. By recognizing that household consumption behavior is a function of the level and composition of income, the set of structural equations can be summarized by a reduced-form equation that expresses household consumption directly as a function of the asset endowments and other exogenous characteristics of the household, and of the economic environment in which it makes decisions. This leads to the following generic estimation equation:

$$\ln E_i = a + bSC_i + cHC_i + dOC_i + eX_i + fZ_i + u_i \tag{1}$$

Where

E_i = household expenditure per capita of household i
SC_i = household endowment of social capital
HC_i = household endowment of human capital
OC_i = household endowment of other assets
X_i = a vector of household characteristics
Z_i = a vector of community/region characteristics
u_i = error term

The key feature of this model is the assumption that social capital is truly capital and hence has a measurable return to the household. This assumption has been the subject of quite a bit of dispute among social scientists. Economists have pointed out that social capital has many features of capital: it requires resources (especially time) to be produced, and it is subject to accumulation and depreciation. The stock of social capital can lead to a stream of benefits which can take many different forms: improved access to credit, improved access to education and health services, improved risk management, etc. However, other economists have pointed at the lack of a market for trading social capital, typical for other types of assets. Some anthropologists have expressed the view that the social phenomena captured by social capital (institutions and networks, and their underlying norms and values) are part of the essential dynamics of a society and should not be reduced to being labeled "capital."

Each analyst needs to determine where he or she stands in terms of accepting this assumption. If it is accepted, the key proposition that can be tested empirically by means of equation (1) is that the networks and organizations to which people belong, and their underlying norms and values, have measurable benefits to these individuals, and lead, directly or indirectly, to a higher level of well-being. The overall impact on well-being can be estimated if the household's consumption level is used as the dependent variable in the equation. The impact on specific aspects of well-being can also be estimated by using other outcome variables as dependent variable: use of education and health services, access to credit, access to agricultural technology and inputs, etc.

A growing number of empirical studies have been undertaken that use equation (1) or variants of it.[13] Perhaps the prime finding from this research has been the large effect of social capital on household welfare. Several studies found that the estimated returns to human capital and social capital are quite similar. In poorer countries, the returns to social capital even tend to exceed those of human capital. There is some evidence to suggest that in such settings social capital acts as a substitute for education. Another important and fairly consistent finding is that the benefits from participating in internally diverse organizations are higher than from participat-

---

13. For a review see Grootaert (2001) and Chapter 3 in Grootaert and van Bastelaer (2002b).

ing in organizations whose members are more alike than different. The reasons for this may have to do with the greater potential for exchanges of knowledge and information and for pooling risks. Members from different backgrounds may indeed have more different knowledge, and may be able to pool risk more effectively because they are more likely to have different sources of income (Grootaert 2001).

One of the important ways in which social capital can contribute to household welfare is by making household enterprises more profitable. For farmers, greater profitability can occur through better access to agricultural technology, inputs, and credit. In the case of trading activities, good networks of clients and suppliers constitute social capital that complements the trader's financial, physical, and human capital. In situations were contract enforcement is often difficult and costly, these networks lower transaction costs and increase profitability. A study of agricultural traders in Madagascar showed that such networks lead to greater sales and value added, and have an effect over and above that of working capital, equipment, labor, and management (Fafchamps and Minten 2002).

Other multivariate studies have attempted to investigate whether social capital improves the non-monetary dimensions of welfare, especially health and education. A study of water supply systems in Central Java, Indonesia, found that social capital had a positive effect on the design, construction, and maintenance of water supply systems in villages, which in turn improved household health. Interestingly, these effects were observed only for piped water systems and not for public wells. It appears that piped water systems require more collective effort and cooperation to construct and maintain, and thus the role of social capital is more critical for their success (Isham and Kahkonen 2002).

Better access to education often holds the key to the next generation's ability to escape from poverty. A higher involvement of the community and parents in the schools can improve the quality of schooling and reduce dropout rates. Coleman (1988) first made this observation about the role of social capital in the acquisition of human capital in the context of U.S. high schools, and it has proved valid in many other countries as well. For example, a study of Burkina Faso used the village average of the number of times households attend parent-teacher association (PTA) meetings as an education-specific indicator of social capital. After controlling for many household and village characteristics, the study found that increased PTA attendance was associated with a significant increase in the probability that children attended school (Grootaert, Oh, and Swami 2002).

Finally, the remaining question is whether social capital helps the poor to the same degree as it does the rich and whether investments in social capital help poor groups escape from poverty. A useful starting point for answering this question is to look at the distribution of the ownership of social capital relative to other types of assets. A study for Bolivia found that social capital is much more equally distributed than physical assets and human capital (Grootaert and Narayan 2000). This means that poor households in Bolivia have relatively more social capital than other assets. This issue can be pursued further by several multivariate techniques. In certain circumstances (for example, when there is significant measurement error in consumption data at the extremes of the distribution), it may be desirable to estimate a probit model of the likelihood of being poor. Studies that have used this method have typically found that social capital significantly reduces the probability of being poor (Grootaert 2001).

One can also explore further whether the role of social capital is different for the poor and the rich. This can be done by means of quantile regressions, which estimate the regression line through given points on the distribution of the dependent variable. Results for several countries have suggested that the returns to social capital are highest at the bottom of the distribution. The same issue can be addressed by splitting the sample according to an exogenous asset variable, such as education or landholdings. This method also indicated for several countries that the returns to social capital were larger for smallholders than for households with higher amounts of land (Grootaert 2001).

The Issue of Endogeneity

All the multivariate methods and results discussed so far depend critically on the assumption that social capital is part of the household's exogenous asset endowment, i.e. those assets that determine income and consumption. This assumption needs to be carefully examined. The formation of networks and associations can be costly in terms of time and other resources. Conceivably, therefore, households with higher income can devote more resources to network formation and thus acquire more social capital more easily. This is not unlike the situation of human capital, the demand for which also increases with income. The possibility exists then, that social capital, like human capital, can be at least partly a consumption good. The extent to which this is the case depends in part on the type of network or association. For example, demand for participation in social groups pursuing leisure activities is quite likely to rise with income because leisure is usually a luxury good. If social capital is in part a consumption good, reverse causality, from welfare level to social capital, is possible. In econometric terms, social capital becomes endogenous, and its estimated coefficient will be upward biased if equation (1) is estimated by Ordinary Least Squares (OLS).

The standard solution to endogeneity problems is the use of instrumental variable estimation, which provides an empirical test of the extent of two-way causality. The real challenge for applying this method is to find a suitable set of instruments for social capital: instruments must determine social capital, but not household welfare (nor be determined by household welfare). It is not an easy task to identify such instruments, and only a limited number of empirical studies have had any measure of success with this approach.[14]

The Determinants of Social Capital

The final question to be addressed with multivariate analysis is what are the determinants of the creation of social capital. Although social capital shares many attributes with other forms of capital, it is fundamentally different in at least one respect, namely, its creation requires interaction between at least two people and usually among a larger group of people. If social capital is not subject to the same person-to-person market exchanges through which, for example, physical capital can be acquired or sold, then how does it come about? The literature has demonstrated that the creation of social capital is a complex process heavily influenced by social, political, and cultural factors as well as by the dominant types of economic activities. The construction of empirical models with social capital as the dependent variable will therefore have to be much more complex than models that merely seek to assess the relative contribution of social capital together with other determinants of well-being. Hence, great caution is needed if data from the SC-IQ are used for multivariate analysis with social capital as the dependent variable. Even when the SC-IQ is combined with an LSMS, which provides information on a large number of socio-economic variables, the number of determinants of the creation of social capital that can actually be captured in a quantitative model based on these data is likely to be a small subset of the total set of relevant variables. At the very least any such model would be subject to significant specification bias. It is likely that the process of creation (and destruction) of social capital will be understood better by means of a variety of qualitative in-depth studies. Quantitative multivariate methods could then be used to test empirically specific aspects of the creation process discovered by the qualitative studies. Examples of this approach can be found in Grootaert and van Bastelaer (2002a).

Reporting and Disseminating Results

As the discussion in the previous section has indicated, the analysis of social capital data can be complex. Extracting the relevant policy messages and conveying them in simple terms to policy makers can represent a distinct challenge. The first issue to be tackled is how to convey the operational

---

14. This issue is further discussed in Chapter 3 of Grootaert and van Bastelaer (2002b). Durlauf (2002) provides a critical review of empirical social capital studies, focused on the endogeneity issue.

meaning of social capital. The literature on social capital is unfortunately strife with a multitude of definitions, many of which are contradictory in terms of what does or does not constitute social capital. This leaves both the casual reader and many experts confused as to what are the most appropriate boundaries for a policy-relevant definition of social capital. It is sometimes helpful to keep the focus on the sector of interest. For example, when a social capital study is undertaken in the context of educational policy reform, the explanation of the concept and the listing of relevant institutions and norms can be confined to those that have a direct bearing on education. Parent-teacher organizations and teacher unions are likely to be more important for education reform than, say, rotating saving and credit associations.

The second challenge is not to overplay the social capital card in the report to policy makers. There have been some valid criticisms that in some reports or studies social capital has been presented as the cure for all development problems. Most of the empirical studies undertaken to date have shown that the effects of social capital are not marginal and often in the same order of magnitude of other determinants of development outcomes, and this finding can legitimately be underscored. However, in almost all cases, the effects of social capital come about because of its synergy with other assets. This is a critical consideration to keep in mind when developing policy recommendations pertaining to social capital.

Almost inevitably, reports to policy makers which point at the strong impacts of social capital will lead to the question how existing social capital can be strengthened and/or how new social capital can be created. It seems fair to say that the social capital literature has been more successful at documenting the beneficial impact of social capital than at deriving policy prescriptions and providing guidelines about how to invest in it. "Investing" in social capital is more difficult than investing in human capital, were a number of time-tested approaches are available (building schools, training teachers, developing appropriate curricula, etc.). Equivalent recommendations for investing in social capital have not yet emerged. When presenting the results of analytic studies based on the SC-IQ or other social capital instruments to policy makers, it is appropriate to be commensurately cautious.

This limitation notwithstanding, the results from well-designed analytic studies on social capital can have several direct bearings on the design of policy and projects. As this paper has hopefully indicated, analytic tools are sufficiently developed to register the presence and forms of social capital in a community. Including this information in project design can lead to development activities that, at a minimum, do not negatively affect existing social structures and norms. Furthermore, the study results can help select between alternative project designs. Information on the existence and forms of social capital in the community can help select the design that will maximize the leveraging role of social capital in influencing project outcomes. In this context, it is important that the social capital assessment exercise is undertaken at an early stage of project design.

Completing the Loop: Feedback for Future Improvements

This document has attempted to explain the origins and rationale for the SC-IQ, and the uses that can be made of the data collected with it. As the text indicated, the SC-IQ draws on a large body of experience with collecting data on social capital, covering more than 15 countries. Nevertheless, it is clear that the SC-IQ should not be seen as the final word on how to collect social capital data. It remains a work in progress. Social capital is a relatively young topic in the social sciences and our conceptual and theoretical understanding continues to develop. In parallel, our ability to measure social capital also continues to increase. Each time the SC-IQ (or another tool for measuring social capital) is applied in the field, lessons will be learned that can improve the tool. It is important that these lessons be shared among researchers and practitioners.

The Social Capital Thematic Group at the World Bank is committed to providing state-of-the-art tools for the measurement and analysis of social capital. We hope therefore that teams applying the SC-IQ would share their experiences with the members of the thematic group, so that we can continue to improve the SC-IQ. To that effect, contact information is provided below. We thank you in advance for using the SC-IQ and for your feedback.

Deepa Narayan
Poverty Reduction and Economic Management Network
The World Bank, 1818 H Street NW
Washington DC 20433, USA
Tel: 202 473 1304, Fax: 202 522 3283
Email: dnarayan@worldbank.org

Veronica Nyhan Jones
Community Empowerment & Social Inclusion, WBI
Poverty Group, PREM
Mailstop J4-400
The World Bank, 1818 H Street NW
Washington, DC 20433 USA
Tel: 202 473-7940 Fax: 202 676-0978
Email: vnyhan@worldbank.org

Michael Woolcock
Development Research Group
Mailstop MC3-306
The World Bank, 1818 H Street NW
Washington, DC 20433 USA
Tel: 202 473-9258   Fax: 202 522-1153
Email: mwoolcock@worldbank.org

For more information on social capital, go to: www.worldbank.org/poverty/scapital

PILOT TESTS IN ALBANIA AND NIGERIA[15]

In the summer of 2002, pilot tests of the SC-IQ were undertaken in Albania and Nigeria. Albania was chosen because there were few cases from Eastern Europe or Central Asia among the major studies that fed into the SC-IQ. Nigeria allowed for testing of different contexts within a very complex country. In both countries, qualified research teams could be identified quickly.

In Albania, a lead researcher was identified who then brought together a team of junior researchers and enumerators to be trained and conduct the pilot. In Nigeria, due to the large country size and the need to conduct the pilot in at least three different languages, three lead researchers were identified (one for each region) and each had a team familiar with the local languages working with them. Importantly, all researchers and enumerators had interest and experience in the social dimensions of development. If this module is being incorporated into a larger household survey, some additional training and sensitization of the enumerators may be required. Typical enumerators may need help understanding and therefore explaining in the field concepts such as trust and empowerment.

Country teams received training prior to conducting the pilot. In Albania, there was a two-day face-to-face workshop with the entire research and field team. Due to resource constraints and the costs associated with traveling across regions, the lead researchers in Nigeria were trained by videoconference in Abuja during a one-day event. These researchers then had to individually train their local enumerators. The training consisted of reviewing the entire survey, question by question, and providing any needed clarifications regarding the intent, or spirit, of the questions, and allowing time for the participants to discuss the most accurate and consistent manner in

15. We are grateful to the local teams who made these field tests possible, including, in Nigeria, Foluso Okinmadewa, Justice Onu, Ibrahim Bayaso, Christopher Raymond, Agatha Tumba, Vivian Taru, Michael Omokoro, Noble J. Nweze, M. A. Adelabu, and in Albania, Ilir Gedeshi, as well as to the enumerators and families who gave their time to participate.

which to express those ideas in local languages. The training also covered the logistics of the questionnaire administration: who would conduct the survey where, with whom, how regions and households would be selected for inclusion in the survey, what the format of the final report would be, etc. To conduct the pilots effectively and responsibly, issues such as building trust and rapport, transparency, managing expectations, and documentation were discussed at length.

In Albania, the questionnaire had been translated and copied for participants prior to the workshop, greatly facilitating the process. The training workshop brought to light several needed adaptations to the prototype questionnaire. Several Albania-specific response categories were added to certain questions (e.g. the 'Fis', a particular form of family network, replaced 'Burial Societies' in question 1.1).

In Nigeria, there were not sufficient funds to translate the survey into all three languages (Ibo, Yoruba and Hausa) ahead of time, so it was agreed that enumerators would have to translate on the spot during the interviews. For the sake of consistency across the country, the lead researchers discussed at length how certain terms should be translated across states so that the survey was as consistent as possible.

In three diverse regions of Albania, 257 surveys were completed in 16 villages. The families within the village were chosen at random from resident lists provided by the commune (local government). In some cases these lists were not available and households were chosen by the enumerators with every attempt at randomness and diversity. In each of the three states of Nigeria (Adamawa, Enugu and Osun), five towns were purposefully chosen across three Senatorial districts. In each town, 20 households were interviewed, for a total sample of 300 households. The team spent between two and three days in each of the towns. At each site, much of the first day was spent on the process of social mapping, listing and identifying the households that would be included in the survey.

Key Findings

Household selection. Significant time and energy should be spent designing and agreeing upon methods for identifying households within a given community and deciding who locally should be engaged to assist with that.

Language. Teams in both countries faced several translation issues. For example, the Nigerian team struggled with the terms 'get along', 'togetherness' and 'fairness'. Also, the question on trust which offers the responses 'most people can be trusted' versus 'you can't be too careful' was difficult to translate.

Time. Nigerian teams required on average two hours to conduct each interview, partly due to the challenge of translating on the spot. In Albania, the average interview time ranged from 30 to 60 minutes. Additional time variance across the countries was due to variation in the respondents' memberships in organizations: Nigerian households were engaged in many more organizations than Albanian households, making the interviewing process more complex.

Adapting specific questions to the local context and sensitivities. This issue came up repeatedly during the training sessions. In some cases, a change was uniformly adopted, e.g. relating to all questions that ask about changes/differences since five years ago. In the Nigerian context, all agreed that it would be more effective to ask about the difference pre- and post-democracy (1999). Similarly in Albania, they preferred to mark time according to pre- and post-refugee influx from Kosovo.

In other cases, specific questions needed adaptation because they could spark embarrassment or suspicion. In Nigeria, several people interpreted the word "drinks" in question 5.10 as alcoholic drinks and they felt embarrassed by it; enumerators thus thought it should be removed. Similarly, in Albania, rural women do not typically meet outside the home as one of the questions on sociability asks.

Question 1.12 [Are members of your group mostly of the same political viewpoint or belong to the same political party?] proved to be very sensitive and it generated suspicion and doubt about the survey. Some saw questions 6.5 [In the past year how often have people in this village/neighborhood gotten together to jointly petition government officials or political leaders for something benefiting the community?] and 6.6 [Were any of these petitions successful?] as confrontational and it led to doubts about the enumerators' claims that they were not with the government. However, other respondents found these (and other political action) questions enlightening, as they were not aware of citizens engaging in such activities. In Nigeria, question 6.3 on changing the course of one's life was frowned at because some respondents believe that only God has the power to do that.

Challenging concepts. Questions relating to empowerment and control over one's life were not easily communicated or understood.

Unanticipated reactions/responses. Because a survey uses closed-ended questions, it can be difficult to anticipate the range of responses and interpretations across local contexts. The pilot helped to uncover some of these. For example, in Nigeria question 1.18 [Does this group work or interact with other groups with similar goals in the village/neighborhood?] was perceived by some respondents as referring to a loss of focus by the leadership of the group as opposed to a strength (in terms of bridging social capital) as it was intended by the survey designers.

Conclusions

Local adaptation, while resource intensive, is essential. A well-done pilot will significantly reduce problems that occur in the field, saving time and money and improving accuracy in the long run. However, the pilot will be only as good as the training provided to the local researchers. It is critical that researchers/enumerators thoroughly understand the concepts included in the survey in order to explain them well to respondents. Uniform translation ahead of time will facilitate this process.

PART II

QUESTIONNAIRE

1. Groups and Networks

1.1 I'd like to start by asking you about the groups or organizations, networks, associations to which you or any member of your household belong. These could be formally organized groups or just groups of people who get together regularly to do an activity or talk about things. As I read the following list of groups, please tell me if anyone in this household belongs to such a group. If yes, tell me which household member is most active in this group, and whether he/she participates actively in the group's decision making.

[NOTE: IF A VILLAGE QUESTIONNAIRE HAS BEEN COMPLETED PRIOR TO THE HOUSEHOLD QUESTIONNAIRE, THE ENUMERATOR CAN USE THE VILLAGE LIST OF GROUPS TO PROBE.]

Type of Organization or Group	Name of Organization or Group	Code of Most Active Household Member [ENUMERATOR: USE CODE NUMBERS FROM HOUSEHOLD ROSTER]	How actively does this person participate in the group's decision making? 1 = Leader 2 = Very Active 3 = Somewhat Active 4 = Does not participate in decision making
A. Farmer/Fisherman group or cooperative			

25

B. Other production group			
C. Traders or Business Association			
D. Professional Association (doctors, teachers, veterans)			
E. Trade Union or Labor Union			
F. Neighborhood/ Village committee			
G. Religious or spiritual group (e.g. church, mosque, temple, informal religious group, religious study group)			
H. Political group or movement			
I. Cultural group or association (e.g. arts, music, theater, film)			
J. Burial society or festival society			
K. Finance, credit or savings group			

L. Education group (e.g. parent-teacher association, school committee)			
M. Health group			
N. Water and waste management group			
O. Sports group			
P. Youth group			
Q. NGO or civic group (e.g. Rotary Club, Red Cross)			
R. Ethnic-based community group			
S. Other groups			

1.2 Compared to five years ago*, do members of your household participate in more or fewer groups or organizations?

[* ENUMERATOR: TIME PERIOD CAN BE CLARIFIED BY SITUATING IT BEFORE/AFTER MAJOR EVENT]

1   More
2   Same number
3   Fewer

1.3 Of all the groups to which members of your household belong, which two are the most important to your household?

[ENUMERATOR: WRITE DOWN NAMES OF GROUPS]

Group 1 _____

Group 2 _____

1.4 How many times in the past 12 months did anyone in this household participate in this group's activities, e.g. by attending meetings or doing group work?

Group 1 [   ]   Group 2 [   ]

1.5 How does one become a member of this group?

1 Born into the group
2 Required to join
3 Invited
4 Voluntary choice
5 Other (specify) _____

Group 1 [   ]   Group 2 [   ]

1.6 How much money or goods did your household contribute to this group in the past 12 months?

Group 1 [   ]   Group 2 [   ]

1.7 How many days of work did your household give to this group in the past 12 months?

Group 1 [   ]   Group 2 [   ]

1.8 What is the main benefit from joining this group?

1 Improves my household's current livelihood or access to services
2 Important in times of emergency/in future
3 Benefits the community
4 Enjoyment/Recreation
5 Spiritual, social status, self-esteem
6 Other (specify) _____

Group 1 [   ]   Group 2 [   ]

1.9 Does the group help your household get access to any of the following services?

1 Yes
2 No

	Group 1	Group 2
A. Education or Training		
B. Health services		
C. Water supply or sanitation		
D. Credit or Savings		
E. Agricultural input or technology		
F. Irrigation		
G. Other (specify)		

1.10 Thinking about the members of this group, are most of them of the same…

1 Yes
2 No

	Group 1	Group 2
A. Neighborhood/Village		
B. Family or Kin group		
C. Religion		
D. Gender		
E. Age		
F. Ethnic or linguistic group/race/ caste/tribe		

1.11 Do members mostly have the same…

1 Yes
2 No

	Group 1	Group 2
A. Occupation		
B. Educational background or level		

1.12 Are members mostly of the same political viewpoint or belong to the same political party?

1 Yes
2 No

Group 1 [   ]   Group 2 [   ]

1.13 Are some members richer or poorer than others, or do they all have mostly the same income level?

1 Mostly same income level
2 Mixed rich/poor

Group 1 [   ]   Group 2 [   ]

1.14 In the past five years*, has membership in the group declined, remained the same, or increased?

[* ENUMERATOR: TIME PERIOD CAN BE CLARIFIED BY SITUATING IT BEFORE/AFTER MAJOR EVENT]

1 Declined
2 Remained same
3 Increased

Group 1   ☐   Group 2   ☐

1.15 When there is a decision to be made in the group, how does this usually come about?

1 Decision is imposed from outside
2 The leader decides and informs the other group members
3 The leader asks group members what they think and then decides
4 The group members hold a discussion and decide together
5 Other (specify _____)

Group 1   ☐   Group 2   ☐

1.16 How are leaders in this group selected?

1 By an outside person or entity
2 Each leader chooses his/her successor
3 By a small group of members
4 By decision/vote of all members
5 Other (specify _____)

Group 1   ☐   Group 2   ☐

1.17 Overall, how effective is the group's leadership?

1 Very effective
2 Somewhat effective
3 Not effective

Group 1   ☐   Group 2   ☐

1.18 Does this group work or interact with other groups with similar goals *in* the village/neighborhood?

1 No
2 Yes, occasionally
3 Yes, frequently

Group 1   ☐   Group 2   ☐

1.19 Does this group work or interact with other groups with similar goals *outside* the village/neighborhood?

1 No
2 Yes, occasionally
3 Yes, frequently

Group 1   ☐   Group 2   ☐

1.20 Does this group work or interact with other groups with different goals *in* the village/neighborhood?

    1 No
    2 Yes, occasionally
    3 Yes, frequently

    Group 1   Group 2

1.21 Does this group work or interact with other groups with different goals *outside* the village/neighborhood?

    1 No
    2 Yes, occasionally
    3 Yes, frequently

    Group 1   Group 2

1.22 What is the most important source of funding of this group?

    1 From members' dues
    2 Other sources within the community
    3 Sources outside the community

    Group 1   Group 2

1.23 What is the most important source of expertise or advice which this group receives?

    1 From within the membership
    2 From other sources within the community
    3 From sources outside the community

    Group 1   Group 2

1.24 Who originally founded the group?

    1 Central government
    2 Local government
    3 Local leader
    4 Community members

    Group 1   Group 2

Networks

1.25 About how many *close* friends do you have these days? These are people you feel at ease with, can talk to about private matters, or call on for help.

1.26 If you suddenly needed a small amount of money [RURAL: enough to pay for expenses for your household for one week; URBAN: equal to about one week's wages], how many people beyond your immediate household could you turn to who would be *willing* to provide this money?

    1 No one
    2 One or two people
    3 Three or four people
    4 Five or more people

1.27 [If not zero] Of those people, how many do you think are currently *able* to provide this money?

```
┌─────────────┐
│             │
└─────────────┘
```

1.28 [If not zero] Are most of these people of similar/higher/lower economic status?

1 Similar
2 Higher
3 Lower

```
┌─────────────┐
│             │
└─────────────┘
```

1.29 If you suddenly had to go away for a day or two, could you count on your neighbors to take care of your children?

1 Definitely
2 Probably
3 Probably not
4 Definitely not

```
┌─────────────┐
│             │
└─────────────┘
```

1.30 If you suddenly faced a long-term emergency such as the death of a breadwinner or [RURAL: harvest failure; URBAN: job loss], how many people beyond your immediate household could you turn to who would be *willing* to assist you?

1 No one
2 One or two people
3 Three or four people
4 Five or more people

```
┌─────────────┐
│             │
└─────────────┘
```

1.31 [If not zero] Of those people, how many do you think are currently *able* to assist you?

```
┌─────────────┐
│             │
└─────────────┘
```

1.32 In the past 12 months, how many people with a personal problem have turned to you for assistance?

```
┌─────────────┐
│             │
└─────────────┘
```

1.33 [If not zero] Are most of these people of similar/higher/lower economic status?

1 Similar
2 Higher
3 Lower

```
┌─────────────┐
│             │
└─────────────┘
```

2. Trust and Solidarity

In every community, some people get along with others and trust each other, while other people do not. Now, I would like to talk to you about trust and solidarity in your community.

2.1 Generally speaking, would you say that most people can be trusted, or that you can't be too careful in your dealings with other people?

1 Most people can be trusted
2 You can't be too careful

```
┌─────────────┐
│             │
└─────────────┘
```

2.2 In general, do you agree or disagree with the following statements?

	1. Agree strongly 2. Agree somewhat 3. Neither agree nor disagree 4. Disagree somewhat 5. Disagree strongly
A. Most people who live in this village/neighborhood can be trusted.	
B. In this village/neighborhood, one has to be alert or someone is likely to take advantage of you.	
C. Most people in this village/neighborhood are willing to help if you need it.	
D. In this village/neighborhood, people generally do not trust each other in matters of lending and borrowing money.	

2.3 Now I want to ask you how much you trust different types of people. On a scale of 1 to 5, where 1 means a very small extent and 5 means a very great extent, how much do you trust the people in that category?

	1. To a very small extent 2. To a small extent 3. Neither small nor great extent 4. To a great extent 5. To a very great extent
A. People from your ethnic or linguistic group/race/caste/tribe	
B. People from other ethnic or linguistic groups/race/caste/tribe	
C. Shopkeepers	
D. Local government officials	
E. Central government officials	
F. Police	
G. Teachers	
H. Nurses and doctors	
I. Strangers	

2.4 Do you think that over the last five years*, the level of trust in this village/neighborhood has gotten better, worse, or stayed about the same?

[* ENUMERATOR: TIME PERIOD CAN BE CLARIFIED BY SITUATING IT BEFORE/AFTER MAJOR EVENT]

1 Gotten better
2 Gotten worse
3 Stayed about the same

2.5 How well do people in your village/neighborhood help each other out these days? Use a five point scale, where 1 means always helping and 5 means never helping.

1   Always helping
2   Helping most of the time
3   Helping sometimes
4   Rarely helping
5   Never helping

2.6 If a community project does not directly benefit you, but has benefits for many others in the village/neighborhood, would you contribute time or money to the project?

A. Time

1   Will not contribute time
2   Will contribute time

B. Money

1   Will not contribute money
2   Will contribute money

3. Collective Action and Cooperation

3.1 In the past 12 months, have you worked with others in your village/neighborhood to do something for the benefit of the community?

1   Yes
2   No → skip to question 3.4

3.2 What were the three main such activities in the past 12 months? Was participation in these voluntary or required?

	Voluntary	Required

3.3 All together, how many days in the past 12 months did you or anyone else in your household participate in community activities?

3.4 How likely is it that people who do not participate in community activities will be criticized or sanctioned?

1   Very likely
2   Somewhat likely
3   Neither likely nor unlikely
4   Somewhat unlikely
5   Very unlikely

3.5 What proportion of people in this village/neighborhood contribute time or money toward common development goals, such as (RURAL: building a levy or repairing a road; URBAN: repairing a road or maintaining a community center)?

1 Everyone
2 More than half
3 About half
4 Less than half
5 No one

3.6 If there was a water supply problem in this community, how likely is it that people will cooperate to try to solve the problem?

1 Very likely
2 Somewhat likely
3 Neither likely or unlikely
4 Somewhat unlikely
5 Very unlikely

3.7 Suppose something unfortunate happened to someone in the village/neighborhood, such as a serious illness, or the death of a parent. How likely is it that some people in the community would get together to help them?

1 Very likely
2 Somewhat likely
3 Neither likely or unlikely
4 Somewhat unlikely
5 Very unlikely

4. Information and Communication

4.1 How long does it take you to reach the nearest working post office?

1 Less than 15 minutes
2 15-30 minutes
3 31-60 minutes
4 More than one hour

4.2 How many times in the last month have you or anyone in your household read a newspaper or had one read to you?

4.3 How often do you listen to the radio?

1 Every day
2 A few times a week
3 Once a week
4 Less than once a week
5 Never

4.4 How often do you watch television?

1 Every day
2 A few times a week
3 Once a week
4 Less than once a week
5 Never

4.5 How long does it take you to get to the nearest working telephone?

1 Telephone in the house
2 Less than 15 minutes
3 15-30 minutes
4 31-60 minutes
5 More than 1 hour

4.6 In the past month, how many times have you made or received a phone call?

4.7 What are the three most important sources of information about what the government is doing (such as agricultural extension, workfare, family planning, etc.)?

1   Relatives, friends and neighbors
2   Community bulletin board
3   Local market
4   Community or local newspaper
5   National newspaper
6   Radio
7   Television
8   Groups or associations
9   Business or work associates
10 Political associates
11 Community leaders
12 An agent of the government
13 NGOs
14 Internet

4.8 What are the three most important sources of market information (such as jobs, prices of goods or crops)?

1   Relatives, friends and neighbors
2   Community bulletin board
3   Local market
4   Community or local newspaper
5   National newspaper
6   Radio
7   Television
8   Groups or associations
9   Business or work associates
10 Political associates
11 Community leaders
12 An agent of the government
13 NGOs
14 Internet

4.9 In general, compared to five years ago*, has access to information improved, deteriorated, or stayed about the same?

[* ENUMERATOR: TIME PERIOD CAN BE CLARIFIED BY SITUATING IT BEFORE/AFTER MAJOR EVENT]

1 Improved
2 Deteriorated
3 Stayed about the same

4.10 What part of the year is your house easily accessible by road?

1 All year long
2 Only during certain seasons
3 Never easily accessible

4.11 How many times have you traveled to [RURAL: a neighboring village or town; URBAN: another part of the city] in the past 12 months?

5. Social Cohesion and Inclusion

5.1 How strong is the feeling of togetherness or closeness in your village/neighborhood? Use a five point scale where 1 means feeling very distant and 5 means feeling very close.

1 Very distant
2 Somewhat distant
3 Neither distant nor close
4 Somewhat close
5 Very close

5.2 There are often differences in characteristics between people living in the same village/neighborhood. For example, differences in wealth, income, social status, ethnic background, race, caste, or tribe. There can also be differences in religious or political beliefs, or there can be differences due to age or sex. To what extent do any such differences characterize your village/neighborhood? Use a five point scale where 1 means to a very great extent and 5 means to a very small extent.

1 To a very great extent
2 To a great extent
3 Neither great nor small extent
4 To a small extent
5 To a very small extent

5.3 Do any of these differences cause problems?

1 Yes
2 No → go to question 5.6

5.4 Which two differences most often cause problems?

1 Differences in education
2 Differences in landholding
3 Differences in wealth/material possessions
4 Differences in social status
5 Differences between men and women
6 Differences between younger and older generations
7 Differences between long-term and recent residents
8 Differences in political party affiliations
9 Differences in religious beliefs
10 Differences in ethnic background/
 race/caste/tribe
11 Other differences

5.5 Have these problems ever led to violence?

1 Yes
2 No

5.6 Are there groups of people in the village/neighborhood who are prevented from or do not have access to any of the following?

	1 Yes 2 No	How many are excluded? 1 Only a few people 2 Many people, but less than half of the village/neighborhood 3 More than half the village/neighborhood
A. Education/schools		
B. Health services/clinics		
C. Water		
D. Justice		
E. Transportation		

5.7 Are there any community activities in which you are not allowed to participate?

1 Yes
2 No, I can participate in all
 activities → skip to question 5.10

5.8 In which activities are you not allowed to participate?
 [ENUMERATOR: LIST UP TO 3 ACTIVITIES]

5.9 Why are you not allowed to participate?

[ENUMERATOR: LIST UP TO 2 REASONS]


```
┌─────────────┐
│             │
└─────────────┘
┌─────────────┐
│             │
└─────────────┘
```

1 Poverty
2 Occupation
3 Lack of education
4 Gender
5 Age
6 Religion
7 Political affiliation
8 Ethnicity or language spoken/race/caste/tribe
9 Other (specify _____)

Sociability

I am now going to ask a few questions about your everyday social interactions.

5.10 In the last month, how many times have you met with people in a public place either to talk or to have food or drinks?

5.11 In the last month, how many times have people visited you in your home?

5.12 In the last month, how many times have you visited people in their home?

5.13 Were the people you met and visited with mostly...

	1 Yes 2 No
A. Of different ethnic or linguistic group/race/caste/tribe	
B. Of different economic status	
C. Of different social status	
D. Of different religious group	

5.14 In the last three months, how many times have you gotten together with people to play games, sports, or other recreational activities?

5.15 How many times in the past 12 months did you participate in a family/village/ neighbor-
hood festival or ceremony (wedding, funeral, religious festival, etc.)?

Conflict and Violence

5.16 In your opinion, is this village/neighborhood generally peaceful or marked by violence?

1 Very peaceful
2 Moderately peaceful
3 Neither peaceful nor violent
4 Moderately violent
5 Very violent

5.17 Compared to five years ago*, has the level of violence in this village/neighborhood
increased, decreased, or stayed the same?

[* ENUMERATOR: TIME PERIOD CAN BE CLARIFIED BY SITUATING IT BEFORE/AFTER MAJOR
EVENT]

1 Increased a lot
2 Increased a little
3 Stayed about the same
4 Decreased a little
5 Decreased a lot

5.18 In general, how safe from crime and violence do you feel when you are alone at home?

1 Very safe
2 Moderately safe
3 Neither safe nor unsafe
4 Moderately unsafe
5 Very unsafe

5.19 How safe do you feel when walking down your street alone after dark?

1 Very safe
2 Moderately safe
3 Neither safe nor unsafe
4 Moderately unsafe
5 Very unsafe

5.20 In the past 12 months, have you or anyone in your household been the victim of a violent
crime, such as assault or mugging?

1 Yes
2 No → go to question 5.22

5.21 How many times?

5.22 In the past 12 months, has your house been burglarized or vandalized?

1 Yes
2 No → go to question 6.1

5.23 How many times?

6. Empowerment and Political Action

6.1 In general, how happy do you consider yourself to be?

1 Very happy
2 Moderately happy
3 Neither happy nor unhappy
4 Moderately unhappy
5 Very unhappy

6.2 How much control do you feel you have in making decisions that affect your everyday activities? Do you have…

1 No control
2 Control over very few decisions
3 Control over some decisions
4 Control over most decisions
5 Control over all decisions

6.3 Do you feel that you have the power to make important decisions that change the course of your life? Rate yourself on a 1 to 5 scale, where 1 means being totally unable to change your life, and five means having full control over your life.

1 Totally unable to change life
2 Mostly unable to change life
3 Neither able nor unable
4 Mostly able to change life
5 Totally able to change life

6.4 Overall, how much impact do you think you have in making this village/neighborhood a better place to live?

1 A big impact
2 A small impact
3 No impact

6.5 In the past 12 months, how often have people in this village/neighborhood gotten together to jointly petition government officials or political leaders for something benefiting the community?

1 Never → skip to question 6.7
2 Once
3 A few times (≤ 5)
4 Many times (> 5)

6.6 Were any of these petitions successful?

1 Yes, all were successful
2 Most were successful
3 Most were unsuccessful
4 None were successful

6.7 In the past 12 months, have you done any of the following?

	1 Yes 2 No
A. Attend a village/neighborhood council meeting, public hearing, or public discussion group	
B. Met with a politician, called him/her, or sent a letter	
C. Participated in a protest or demonstration	
D. Participated in an information or election campaign	
E. Alerted newspaper, radio or TV to a local problem	
F. Notified police or court about a local problem	

6.8 Lots of people find it difficult to get out and vote. Did you vote in the last local election?

1 Yes
2 No

6.9 Did you vote in the last state/national/presidential election?

1 Yes
2 No

6.10 Would you ever vote for a candidate who was not from your ethnic or linguistic group/race/caste/tribe?

1 Yes
2 No

6.11 To what extent do local government and local leaders take into account concerns voiced by you and people like you when they make decisions that affect you?

1 A lot
2 A little
3 Not at all

6.12 In your opinion, how honest are the officials and staff of the following agencies? Please rate them on a 1 to 5 scale, where 1 is very dishonest and 5 is very honest.

	1 Very dishonest 2 Mostly dishonest 3 Neither honest nor dishonest 4 Mostly honest 5 Very honest 9 Not applicable (agency not in village/neighborhood)
A. Local government officials	
B. Traditional village leaders	
C. Doctors and nurses in health clinic	
D. Teachers and school officials	
E. Staff of post office	
F. Police	
G. Judges and staff of courts	
H. Staff of NGOs	

6.13 In general, compared to five years ago*, has the honesty of local government improved, deteriorated, or stayed about the same?
[* ENUMERATOR: TIME PERIOD CAN BE CLARIFIED BY SITUATING IT BEFORE/AFTER MAJOR EVENT]

1 Improved
2 Deteriorated
3 Stayed about the same

6.14 In the past 12 months, did your household have to pay some additional money to government officials to get things done?

1 Yes, often
2 Yes, occasionally
3 No → end interview

6.15 Are such payments effective in getting a service delivered or a problem solved?

1 Yes, usually
2 Yes, but only occasionally
3 Usually not

CORE QUESTIONS[16]

Groups and Networks

1. I would like to start by asking you about the groups or organizations, networks, associations to which you or any member of your household belong. These could be formally organized groups or just groups of people who get together *regularly* to do an activity or talk about things. Of how many such groups are you or any one in your household a member?

2. Of all these groups to which you or members of your household belong, which one is the most important to your household?

_____ [Name of group]

3. Thinking about the members of this group, are most of them of the same....

	1 Yes 2 No
A. Religion	
B. Gender	
C. Ethnic or linguistic background/ race/caste/tribe	

---

16. For a more limited range of questionnaire items to be included in a shorter survey, the following 27 questions, drawn from the longer list above, are those we deem to be most essential.

45

4. Do members mostly have the same...

	1 Yes 2 No
A. Occupation	
B. Educational background or level	

5. Does this group work with or interact with groups *outside* the village/neighborhood?

   1. No
   2. Yes, occasionally
   3. Yes, frequently

6. About how many *close friends* do you have these days? These are people you feel at ease with, can talk to about private matters, or call on for help.

7. If you suddenly needed to borrow a small amount of money [RURAL: enough to pay for expenses for your household for one week; URBAN: equal to about one week's wages], are there people beyond your immediate household and close relatives to whom you could turn and who would be willing and able to provide this money?

   1. Definitely
   2. Probably
   3. Unsure
   4. Probably not
   5. Definitely not

Trust and Solidarity

8. Generally speaking, would you say that most people can be trusted or that you can't be too careful in dealing with people?

   1. People can be trusted
   2. You can't be too careful

9. In general, do you agree or disagree with the following statements?

	1 Agree strongly 2 Agree somewhat 3 Neither agree or disagree 4 Disagree somewhat 5 Disagree strongly
A. Most people in this village/neighborhood are willing to help if you need it.	
B. In this village/neighborhood, one has to be alert or someone is likely to take advantage of you.	

10. How much do you trust....

	1 To a very great extent 2 To a great extent 3 Neither great nor small extent 4 To a small extent 5 To a very small extent
A. Local government officials	
B. Central government officials	

11. If a community project does not directly benefit you but has benefits for many others in the village/neighborhood, would you contribute time or money to the project?

   A. Time   [　　　]   B. Money   [　　　]

   1 Will not contribute time   1 Will not contribute money
   2 Will contribute time   2 Will contribute money

Collective Action and Cooperation

12. In the past 12 months did you or any one in your household participate in any communal activities, in which people came together to do some work for the benefit of the community?

   1. Yes
   2. No (skip to question 14)   [　　　]

13. How many times in the past 12 months?

   [　　　]

14. If there was a water supply problem in this community, how likely is it that people will cooperate to try to solve the problem?

   1. Very likely
   2. Somewhat likely
   3. Neither likely or unlikely
   4. Somewhat unlikely
   5. Very unlikely   [　　　]

Information and Communication

15. In the past month, how many times have you made or received a phone call?

   [　　　]

16. What are your three main sources of information about what the government is doing (such as agricultural extension, workfare, family planning, etc.)?

   1. Relatives, friends and neighbors
   2. Community bulletin board
   3. Local market
   4. Community or local newspaper
   5. National newspaper
   6. Radio
   7. Television

   8. Groups or associations
   9. Business or work associates
   10. Political associates
   11. Community leaders
   12. An agent of the government
   13. NGOs
   14. Internet

Social Cohesion and Inclusion

17. There are often differences in characteristics between people living in the same village/neighborhood. For example, differences in wealth, income, social status, ethnic or linguistic background/race/caste/tribe. There can also be differences in religious or political beliefs, or there can be differences due to age or sex. To what extent do any such differences characterize your village/neighborhood? Use a five point scale where 1 means to a very great extent and 5 means to a very small extent.

   1. To a very great extent
   2. To a great extent
   3. Neither great nor small extent
   4. To a small extent
   5. To a very small extent

18. Do any of these differences cause problems?

   1. Yes
   2. No → go to question 21.

19. Which two differences most often cause problems?

   1. Differences in education
   2. Differences in landholding
   3. Differences in wealth/material possessions
   4. Differences in social status
   5. Differences between men and women
   6. Differences between younger and older generations
   7. Differences between long-term and recent residents
   8. Differences in political party affiliations
   9. Differences in religious beliefs
   10. Differences in ethnic or linguistic background/
       race/caste/tribe
   11. Other differences

20. Have these problems ever led to violence?

   1. Yes
   2. No

21. How many times in the past month have you got together with people to have food or drinks, either in their home or in a public place?

22. [IF NOT ZERO] Were any of these people....

	1 Yes 2 No
A. Of different ethnic or linguistic background/ race/caste/tribe?	
B. Of different economic status?	
C. Of different social status?	
D. Of different religious groups?	

23. In general, how safe from crime and violence do you feel when you are alone at home?

1. Very safe
2. Moderately safe
3. Neither safe nor unsafe
4. Moderately unsafe
5. Very unsafe

Empowerment and Political Action
24. In general, how happy do you consider yourself to be?

1. Very happy
2. Moderately happy
3. Neither happy nor unhappy
4. Moderately unhappy
5. Very unhappy

25. Do you feel that you have the power to make important decisions that change the course of your life? Rate yourself on a 1 to 5 scale, were 1 means being totally unable to change your life, and 5 means having full control over your life.

1. Totally unable to change life
2. Mostly unable to change life
3. Neither able nor unable
4. Mostly able to change life
5. Totally able to change life

26. In the past 12 months, how often have people in this village/neighborhood got together to jointly petition government officials or political leaders for something benefiting the community?

1. Never
2. Once
3. A few times (<5)
4. Many times (>5)

27. Lots of people find it difficult to get out and vote. Did you vote on the last state/national/ presidential election?

1. Yes
2. No

REFERENCES

Burt, Ronald. 2000. "The Network Structure of Social Capital." In Robert Sutton and Barry Staw, eds. *Research in Organizational Behavior.* Greenwich, CT: JAI Press, pp. 345-423.

Coleman, James. 1988. "Social Capital in the Creation of Human Capital." *American Journal of Sociology* 94 (Supplement): S95-S120.

Collier, Paul. 2002. "Social Capital and Poverty: A Microeconomic Perspective." In Christiaan Grootaert and Thierry van Bastelaer, eds. *The Role of Social Capital in Development: An Empirical Assessment.* New York: Cambridge University Press, pp. 19-41.

Durlauf, Stephen. 2002. "On the Empirics of Social Capital." *Economic Journal* 112 (483): 459-479.

Fafchamps, Marcel, and Bart Minten. 2002. "Social Capital and the Firm: Evidence from Agricultural Traders in Madagascar." In Christiaan Grootaert and Thierry van Bastelaer, eds. *The Role of Social Capital in Development: An Empirical Assessment.* New York: Cambridge University Press, pp. 125-54.

Fukuyama, Francis. 1995. *Trust: The Social Virtues and the Creation of Prosperity.* New York: Free Press.

Gittell, Ross and Avis Vidal. 1998. *Community Organizing: Building Social Capital as a Development Strategy.* Newbury Park, CA: Sage Publications.

Glaeser, Edward, David Laibson, and Bruce Sacerdote. 2002. "An Economic Approach to Social Capital." *Economic Journal* 112 (483): 437-458.

Grootaert, Christiaan. 1999. "Social Capital, Household Welfare, and Poverty in Indonesia." Policy Research Working Paper 2148. Washington D.C.: World Bank.

Grootaert, Christiaan. 2001. "Does Social Capital Help the Poor? A Synthesis of Findings from the Local Level Institutions Studies in Bolivia, Burkina Faso, and Indonesia." Local Level Institutions Working Paper 10. World Bank, Social Development Department, Washington D.C.

Grootaert, Christiaan, and Deepa Narayan. 2000. "Local Institutions, Poverty, and Household Welfare in Bolivia." Local Level Institutions Working Paper 9. World Bank, Social Development Department, Washington D.C.

Grootaert, Christiaan, Gi-Taik Oh, and Anand Swami. 2002. "Social Capital, Education and Credit Markets: Empirical Evidence from Burkina Faso." In Jonathan Isham, Thomas Kelly, and Sunder Ramaswamy, eds. *Social Capital and Economic Development: Well-being in Developing Countries*. Cheltenham, UK: Edward Elgar, pp. 85-103.

Grootaert, Christiaan, and Thierry van Bastelaer, eds. 2002a. The Role of Social Capital in *Development: An Empirical Assessment*. New York: Cambridge University Press.

Grootaert, Christiaan, and Thierry van Bastelaer, eds. 2002b. *Understanding and Measuring Social Capital: A Multidisciplinary Tool for Practitioners*. Washington D.C.: World Bank.

Grosh, Margaret, and Paul Glewwe, eds. 2000. *Designing Household Survey Questionnaires for Developing Countries: Lessons from 15 years of the Living Standards Measurement Study*. Washington D.C.: World Bank.

Ibáñez, Ana Maria, Kathy Lindert, and Michael Woolcock. 2002. "Social Capital in Guatemala: A Mixed Methods Analysis." Technical Background Paper No. 12, prepared for the *Guatemala Poverty Assessment*. Washington, D.C.: The World Bank.

Isham, Jonathan, and Satu Kahkonen. 2002. "How Do Participation and Social Capital Affect Community-Based Water Projects? Evidence from Central Java, Indonesia." In Christiaan Grootaert and Thierry van Bastelaer, eds. *The Role of Social Capital in Development: An Empirical Assessment*. New York: Cambridge University Press, pp. 155-187.

Isham, Jonathan, Thomas Kelly, and Sunder Ramaswamy. 2002. "Social capital and well-being in developing countries: an introduction." In Jonathan Isham, Thomas Kelly, and Sunder Ramaswamy, eds. *Social Capital and Economic Development: Well-Being in Developing Countries*. Northampton, MA: Edward Elgar, pp. 3-17.

Jha, Saumitra, Vijayendra Rao and Michael Woolcock. 2002. "Governance in the Gullies: Political Networks and Leadership Among Delhi's Urban Poor." Paper presented at Economists Forum. Washington, DC: World Bank.

Krishna, Anirudh. 2002. *Active Social Capital: Tracing the Roots of Development and Democracy*. New York: Columbia University Press.

Krishna, Anirudh, and Norman Uphoff. 2002. "Mapping and Measuring Social Capital Through Assessment of Collective Action for Conserve and Develop Watersheds in Rajasthan, India." In Christiaan Grootaert and Thierry van Bastelaer, eds. *The Role of Social Capital in Development: An Empirical Assessment*. New York: Cambridge University Press, pp. 85-124.

Narayan, Deepa. 2000. *Voices of the Poor: Can Anyone Hear Us?* New York: Oxford University Press.

Narayan, Deepa. 2002. "Bonds and Bridges: Social Capital and Poverty." In Jonathan Isham, Thomas Kelly, and Sunder Ramaswamy, eds. *Social Capital and Economic Development: Well-Being in Developing Countries*. Northampton, MA: Edward Elgar, pp. 58-81.

Narayan, Deepa, and Michael Cassidy. 2001. "A Dimensional Approach to Measuring Social Capital: Development and Validation of Social Capital Inventory." *Current Sociology* 49 (2): 49-93.

Narayan, Deepa, and Lant Pritchett. 1999. "Cents and Sociability: Household Income and Social Capital in Rural Tanzania." *Economic Development and Cultural Change* 47(4): 871-97.

Portes, Alejandro. 1998. "Social Capital: Its Origins and Applications in Contemporary Sociology." *Annual Review of Sociology* 24: 1-24.

Pritchett, Lant and Michael Woolcock. "Solutions when the Solution is the Problem: Arraying the Disarray in Development." *World Development* (forthcoming).

Putnam, Robert. 2000. *Bowling Alone: The Collapse and Revival of American Community*. New York: Simon and Schuster.

Rao, Vijayendra and Michael Woolcock. 2003. "Integrating Qualitative and Quantitative Approaches in Program Evaluation." In Francois J. Bourguignon and Luiz Pereira da Silva, eds. *Evaluating the Poverty and Distributional Impact of Economic Policies*. Washington, DC: The World Bank.

Woolcock, Michael. 1998. "Social Capital and Economic Development: Toward a Theoretical Synthesis and Policy Framework." *Theory and Society* 27(2): 151-208.

Woolcock, Michael. 1999. "Managing Risk, Shocks, and Opportunity in Developing Economies: The Role of Social Capital." In Gustav Ranis, ed. *Dimensions of Development.* New Haven, CT: Yale Center for International and Area Studies, pp. 197-212.

Woolcock, Michael, and Deepa Narayan. 2000. "Social Capital: Implications for Development Theory, Research, and Policy." *World Bank Research Observer* 15 (2): 225-50.

World Bank. 2000. *World Development Report 2000/2001: Attacking Poverty.* New York: Oxford University Press.

World Bank. 2002. *Empowerment and Poverty Reduction—A Sourcebook.* Washington D.C.: World Bank.

World Bank. 2003. *Guatemala Poverty Assessment.* Washington D.C.: World Bank.

ville, PA USA
2010

51BV00004B/7/A

Breinigsville, PA USA
23 July 2010
242151BV00004B/7/A